I CAN CHANGE EVERYTHING

WRITTEN BY STEPHANIE TAYLOR · ILLUSTRATED BY LAURA BRENLLA

To Alice, Eleanor, Sabine, and Clara,
little change-makers with great big hearts —S. T.

To Martín, the new arrival who makes us want to create a better world,
and his mom, who is already doing her part —L. B.

Text copyright 2019 by Stephanie Taylor
Illustration copyright 2019 by Laura Brenlla

Printed in the United States of America
First Edition

Published by Strong Arm Press
www.strongarmpress.com
Washington, DC
ISBN-13: 978-1-947492-32-5

STRONG
ARM
PRESS

I am powerful!
I can change everything.

I can change the clothes I wear.

I can change my socks and shoes.

I can change my underwear.

I can change my look.
I can wear a smart disguise.
I'm wearing glasses twice
my size!

I can change my hand into a turkey.

I can change a seed into a tree.

I can change a rainy day into

a day at sea.

I can change a hole into a star.

I can change a sandbox into Mars.

I can change my thumbs
into wiggling little people!

By making dots for eyes
and mouths.

I can snap my fingers and change the clouds.

Just watch.

Snap

Snap

What shape are the clouds now?

I can change myself into a mirror with a friend, I can show them how they look and sound.

I can say their words and dance around.
I can make faces back at them.

I can change my voice from soft to loud.

I can change a secret to a very loud shout.

I can shout from the rooftops.

Hear me shout.

I can change myself from being shy.

I can make myself say hi.

I can say goodbye even when it's hard.

I can change the sky into the ground.

I can plant my feet on the clouds.
I can hold the sky up with my feet.

There are new
things I can try.

I can do them over
                    until I get them right.

I can change my feelings into words.
I can change my ideas
into things.

I can change my
pictures into dreams.

Here is what I can't change:
I can't change the color of my eyes.
I can't change my big heart.

But I can change the WORLD!

ACTIVITY PAGES

1. My own list of things I want to change:

- ....
- ....
- ....
- ....
- ....
- ....
- ....
- ....

2. I can change a circle into...

a smiling
face!

a diamond
ring!

a map
of
the Earth!

a ferris
wheel!

How else can the circle change?

CPSIA information can be obtained
at www.ICGtesting.com
Printed in the USA
LVHW071808061219
639529LV00002B/4/P